PILGRIMAGE

A TOUR OF NORTHUMBERLAND IN PICTURES AND POEMS

STAN BECKENSALL

FONTHILL

Supported by

Northumberland National Park

Northumberland National Park was officially designated on the 6th April 1956 and covers an area of 1,049km, or 405 square miles of diverse and inspiring landscapes which contain evocative reminders of a rich and often turbulent past. These can be experienced by visiting the well preserved prehistoric landscapes of the Cheviot Hills in the north, towards Kielder Water and Forest Park in the west then south to Hadrian's Wall World Heritage Site. Criss-crossed by 700 miles of footpaths and rights of way, you can walk, cycle or horse ride with only the sounds of nature for company whilst you explore the beautiful wildlife, natural beauty and rich cultural heritage that lie at the heart of the park, with hidden gems waiting to be discovered.

We have the cleanest air, the cleanest rivers and have been officially recognised for having the darkest skies in England as Northumberland National Park alongside Kielder Water and Forest Park has the prestigious status of being England's first and Europe's largest International Dark Sky Park.

Northumberland National Park truly is full of unforgettable experiences and everlasting memories.

Fonthill Media Limited

First published in the United Kingdom 2014

ISBN 978-1-78155-436-4

Typeset in Adobe Garamond Pro 11/15

Printed and bound in England

Contents

Preface by Kim Cowie

In a life beset by consumerism and the crushing mediocrity of the world's response to natural, economic, social and financial disasters the landscape of Northumberland remains constant, dependable and known. But her glory lies in the paradox of the ever-changing, the unknown and the reckless, ultimately defined only by the seasons.

One man knows that landscape and her people, both ancient and modern, better than any other: Stan Beckensall. This is a collection of words and poems though which Stan tells the story of Northumberland and his journey from past to present. Each creates such a sense of place and belonging that you could believe you were walking the landscape as he created them. Stan invites you to join him on that journey, a journey of the imagination, yet rooted deep in the very earth of Northumberland.

Suspend your worries, leave your technology behind you and step back in time when "instead of hearing, one listened; instead of seeing, one looked; instead of tasting, one savoured; instead of touching, one felt. 'Listen' said, St Benedict, listen with the ear of your heart'* (*The Morville House* by Katherine Swift)

This is a book to soothe ragged nerves, a book to meditate upon, a book to capture what it feels like to belong to a place. Maybe you are new to Northumberland, visiting for the first time, maybe your family has roots deep in her soil. Maybe you are yet to visit. This book makes no judgements, it simply welcomes you in. But once you embark upon this journey be warned, you will be lost. Near or far you will belong to Northumberland.

Pilgrimage

'Pilgrimage' evolved as a journey to a special place reputed to have power to help people in many different ways. In early Christian times the place was associated with someone who had great power to transform life for others. To do so, the object of devotion had to have been someone very special who had done something that would have a great effect on the lives of others. We think of 'saints' as having such power, of people who would intercede with God for us, like Saint Cuthbert or Saint Aidan.

The term is now used widely to refer to a special journey that one makes physically or spiritually. Place and the power of place go together.

I put it this way in one of my books: 'Places generate feelings; some do this because we have learnt what happened there, some because they are physically striking or beautiful, and others because they have some indefinable attraction and quality.'

I first came to Northumberland in 1966 to help train teachers at Alnwick College of Education. Prior to that I had been a head of English in High Schools in Sussex and Malta, after graduating at Keele University and being a National Service Education Officer in the RAF in Norfolk. The place where I spent my early years was Stoke-On-Trent, surrounded by active bottle ovens, coal mines, iron and steel works and other industries. As a boy I used to escape this, especially in camping with a local scout troop and in the numerous parks available then.

Coming to Northumberland was like finding my home after all those years – such a contrast to the place of my birth. I have been constantly aware of how much there is to know about a part of England to which I accidentally came to belong, and my delight in exploring the richness of place and past has led me to publish many books. In this exploration I have become a pilgrim, and my poetry and prose, supported by photography, have drawn me closer to where I now live. I now regard Northumberland as home, not through birth, but because I have earned it.

The poems have been arranged numerically and geographically as a route taken by a pilgrim

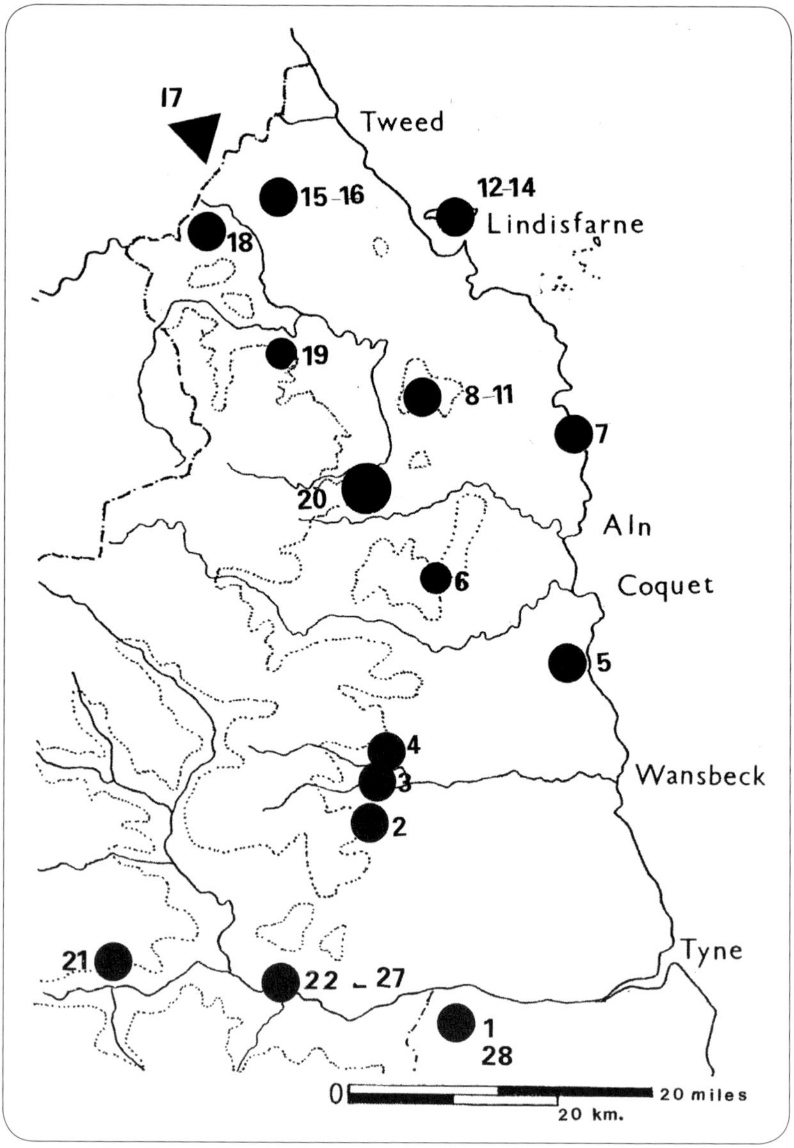

The Angel of the North (Joe Cowie)

The Angel of the North, a public sculpture created by Antony Gormley, on land south of Northumberland, is now one of the best-known of its type in Britain. It rises on land that was once riddled with coal mines. It is a reminder of an industrial past.

Wings outstretched, veins running into the earth, it is representative of Northumbria, and welcomes us to explore the more modern county of Northumberland

1. Angel of the North

High above the roar of motorway,
Holding in an iron head a history
Of coal, bricks, glass and steel,
An Angel pulses life through heavy feet
Firmly anchored in the earth.

Wings shooting sideways welcome our return
Or rise in benediction far above our heads.
No harps of gold or feather flutter,
Haloed hair, drained face
But power immeasurable roaring to the sky,
Rust reality, time battling with time,
A future Ozymandias of the North.

We look, and we despair.
Memorial to pride, our Angel's pivot
Built above black veins and arteries
Scoured out for vital coal,
Feeding the lives of whole communities
Rich with love, with hate, with temperance and booze,
With young men siphoned off from time to time
To feed the nation's need for death in battle,
Where lungs ruined by the dust of ages
Ended with a rattle.
Bairns hopscotched, washing hung in smutted lines,
Where here and there a lonely woman
Waited at her door – a tragic, hopeless expectation.
Our Angel offers openly a truth about our past.

Materials that revolutionized the north
Now constitute the rooted Angel that will never fly,
Except in our imagination.
Power restrained, yet latent, terrifying power,
A paradox of stillness and activity
Ribbed vertically from earth to heaven,
Wings breaking out, it is a metaphor
Of all that we have been, are now, and what we may become.

Oh yes, it tells us life is hard;
Landscapes, all around transformed by forces
Which have dug beneath the earth to clothe its crust
Come with a price: for there is misery and death
And broken limbs, the sacrifice we had to make.
Our eyes look inward through our bodies and our minds
For a moment that is forever still and silent.
Yet a sunset warms the Angel
With a reassurance of another life
Not in the distant future – here and now-
That dull metal forged with skill
Can make the everyday become a work of art,
Bring for a moment heaven to earth,
Extract with a refining fire the good from bad,
And give a solid basis for our hope.

1. *Shaftoe cairn*

There are, and have been, thousands of burial cairns from prehistory of many variations, from communal burials to the burial of an individual in many types of circular mounds.

Cairns
Stamped with lichen, bound by bracken root,
Sunk in acid soil,
Each heap of stone affects disguise.
Death's ritual leaves slight signs.
Slanting sunlight, morning, evening,
Shadows each circumference. Betrays.
Many gouged by curiosity and greed.
First in rank and ostentation – first to fall;
The unpretentious huddle humbly in the soil, survive.
They are the scanty evidence of another life.
A smear upon the soil,
Burnt bone, a piece of flint, a pot, a bead,
Sealed once, but not invulnerable.
We focus on these tiny scraps of time
With force that hurls jet fighters overhead
And simulates the power of sun.
We are our Age, we bring technology
To bear upon a past where writing played no part,
But symbolism loomed large.

Gods lived and were placated;
Man and woman not enough.
Force drove through grass blades, crackled in the skies,
Hurled rainbows, hid the face of moon and sun.

Awesome. Kept us in our place.
We are the piece of broken bone, the pile of dust.
A piece of flint is our technology,
A bead or two our power or vanity.

We are the hands that placed the pot inside the grave,
Love that mourns a while.
The cairn above our heads cuts out the sky
As we move on.

A burial cist (Birtley Aris)

Desertion

There is both beauty and sadness in deserted places. Changes in economics, disease, and politics establish which places will survive. In rural Northumberland these places may have almost disappeared, grown over and returned to the earth, but some of their stories might still be read in the landscape and in documents. History tends to be about the rich and the famous, but we meet the life of simpler people, those who were the majority of the population.

'Lost villages' reveal a vibrant life that was lost

A fine survival is at Middleton, particularly when seen from the air.

2. Deserted Village: Middleton

Sunshine, moonlight, wind-blown sand
May resurrect a village long-since dead and buried.
Crinkled in lush pastures, walling struggles to
Re-create the pattern formed by villagers now dead.
Gardens that once provided food or sustained a cow
Are covered now with close-cropped grass,
With sheep no longer shunted off the cottage plots.
Main street, green, divides the cottage rows
And Rigg and Furrow bend inverted s-shapes
Like a giant comb that halts behind the garths.
Deep furrows hold the shadow-shapes that once grew grain
And drained the earth, now filled with thistledown and reeds.

A map of many lives, of many skills,
Made more dramatic seen from above
Forget uncanny silences: you'll hear again the raucous singing
When the last ear of corn is cut and harvest taken home.
Forget the fossil stillness of the soil.
Listen to the cry of ploughman to his ox.
Forget abandonment of places such as these.
Re-people all.
Recall varieties of trades and self-sufficiency when this was a reality.
The people's past may be beyond the reach of modern man,
Except when slender documents survive.
So learn to read the silent undulations in the land
That may be all that's left to us to share their lives.

Middleton (Newcastle University)

I wrote a book called 'Shadows of the Past', which is inspired by fragments that help to build up a historical record, as our knowledge of the past can only be partial. One source of our knowledge is from gravestones, and Hartburn church has particularly fine examples.

3. Shadows: Hartburn

I meet these insubstantial dwellers of the past,
Shadows which hover over graves that bear their names
Which intermittent sunlight throws into relief.
Testament of life lived long ago in joy or grief and all that lies between
Ending with hope of resurrection, hope of bliss to come.
Here is a microcosm of all history;
Recorded accidents, death of babies, proud longevity.
Each stone quarried from a living rock,
Some words that hide a depth of suffering or pride.
They stand as silent sentinels, but some have toppled into grass,
Wear coverings of moss below a canopy of branches
Or thick darkness of some ancient yew.
A serpent swallowing its tail - a symbol of eternity.
A fading hour-glass holds no sand
Yet still proclaims our time is running out.
A book of life lies open at the page that we would wish most to forget.
Skull grins above a necklace of crossed bones, stripping people to the core.
Urns and frilly curtains are more comfortable reassurances,
Words woven into verse keep loss at bay-
We do not die, but pass away.
A shouldered scythe has cut the harvest of our souls.
Stone angels wait where Godhead sits in judgement on his throne.

When sites were being sought recently for the disposal of nuclear waste, Druridge Bay on the Northumberland coast was a candidate, which raised great opposition

4. Druridge

Earth is a dry ridge, sediment of seas,
A breaker's yard of shell and bone and clay
Transformed to sun-soaked hollows,
Rippling light and shadow dance
Where flowers' heads splash colour on the strand.

Once we could only ruffle surfaces
In exploitation of this land.
Now we can move mountains.
Water rolls upon itself;
The sea sheds skins of waste,
Dead, ready to be transformed into another life.

Our future once was traced in scrolls of light,
Or silver streaks that ran in silence to the moon,
Where mystics linked the sea to sky.

Air poses thunder-threat from alabaster clouds,
Mingles with gull-screech, blue-torn passages of jets.
Wind skims dry sand sharply to the sea.

A caterpillar tread and hungry iron jaws
Tear and flatten in a day, carry sand away.
The menace of a glowing core, power of suns,
A self-perpetuating raging fire becomes
A nightmare of split atoms, nightmare of a new creation.

Nature made in us four elements;
Each part of earth, air, water, fire,
Held to be for centuries the cause of all our moods and life,
A link with laws that teach us all to have aspiring minds.
Now we are called upon to use these talents to protect the earth.

Druridge sand dunes

The valley of Edlingham lies north of a sandstone scarp that dominates the lower land to the Cheviot Hills.

5. Autumn Gold: Edlingham

This valley holds the melting point of gold
Here, at this year's end, poised,
Like this scarp of grey sandstone,
Fretted with cold water running down its cheeks,
We tremble at the edge of silence
And the hovering kestrel's path of time.
Below, a shattered castle keep
Blends with deep shadows of rich earth
As sunlight slowly strokes each tree and field.
A subtle shift of texture threads the cooling air
Among the gentle falling of the leaves,
The spinning of winged seeds or sigh of brittle pine.
But far beyond the urgent change
That dying bracken at our feet foretells,
Grey rounded Cheviots snuggle closer to warm clouds,
While all the space between is indistinct,
Simmering in a crucible of westering sun,
Still glowing gold, dark green and brown,
With flames of scarlet licking round.

The store of summer drains away
To leave an aching sadness for the richness that was there.
Cold realisation of our loss
Throbs slowly through the current of our blood;
We touch the solid rock for reassurance
That next year will be the same,

And after that…and after that…
Who knows what follows?
Our bodies cry inside, 'Stay, stay, Come back. Come back'.
Yet even as we watch,
The sun-shift and the lengthened shadows
Drag away the hope
That we can catch and keep the beauty of this place for ever

Edlingham valley

The coast of Northumberland has dramatic settings for some of its many castles. Here at Dunstanburgh is a magnificent ruin.

6. *Dunstanburgh Castle*

Dark Dunstanburgh guards the coast,
Its tattered fingers lingering on a hill;
A sinister farewell, a last despairing clutch
To keep a hand-hold on the land.

Black-backed gulls insanely shriek,
Streaking steep cliffs with white excrement
As comic seals play in the bubbling bay
To their unresponsive audience.

Volcanic blackened basalt still supports
The last remaining seaward-facing wall
While to the north the crescent sand
And green-backed sand-dunes
Smile indifference on a sea
Where once proud ships rode anchor.

Dunstanburgh castle

The Deep Past

The Old Bewick poems are of an area in north Northumberland that is part of a long series of sandstone scarps that curve round from NE to SW as a prominent landscape feature. There is abundant evidence of prehistoric activity, especially at Old Bewick, where animals were hunted and others were led to summer pastures. The soil is poor, but would have supported light scrub and trees. Here people chose to bury their dead and to make some homes. Today there is a quietness, remoteness, superb views across lower land, and a strong sense of special places. I have explored and excavated sites on this scarp, and some of the excavation work led to a novel ('Unquiet Grave') for the teenagers from local High schools who voluntarily worked with me there for four years. The places mean so much to different people. The name 'Blawearie' suggests that the wind blows wearily there.

8. Sunset: Old Bewick Moor

Autumn sun westering;
Fire in amber floods this land.
A distant kestrel floats on air
That draws the eye from gold to violet.
Rocks on hillsides spring to life,
Sheep whiten in encrusted bracken

Where ruts run like inked lines.
Ramparts on hillforts
Raise themselves to catch the fading light,
Their ditches subterranean, black as jet.
Beyond the scarp, the shredded clouds have gathered,
Radiating sunlight, myriads of beams
That roll fields and streams along,
Awakening the river snake
And raking woods with light.
Rough moorland throbs against pale pasture,
Meets mosaics on stone walls:
A life beyond a life: one calm and smooth,
One rifted, broken up and full of mystery.
And at this meeting place
A tilted table rock, absorbing light,
Libating gold from man-made grooves;
Fluidity, concentric circles leaping into life
And fading with the sun-slip down the scarp.
Black rooks erupt above stiff Douglas fir,
Blown fragments from a fire
That drift awhile, and rest.
Like giant wings, the shadows of the night
Beat out the light.
Blawearie House absorbs a depth of red
That hovers in warm air
Before magenta in the sky cries welcome to the stars.

2. Moonlight

Scattered stagnant ponds
Like silver hoof-prints
Diffuse moonlight,
Image intermittent cloud.
Marsh grass shatters, ice-like,
Furze holds bobbing shreds of wool
Plucked from sheep whose coiled horns
Bow to whispers of stained teeth and tongues.
Round-backed boulders stroked with shadow
Hold earth-fast.
Wheel ruts running deeper fade into a far horizon,
Stretching out the moorland to a mystery
In which a sudden fluttering of wings
Or startled cry from sluggish burn or blackened copse
Echoes from a rock-torn cleugh.
Moonlight lies like frost upon a heather-crusted knoll.
Owl hovers, lands on hawthorn bush,
Grey on spiky black.

The north of Britain has thousands of rocks, from outcrops to small broken pieces that are covered with what have become known as cup and ring marks. Although much is known about their location, context and types of decoration, there are still many unanswered questions about their origin, purpose and use. The Newcastle University website of my research into this once-neglected phenomenon has achieved over 17 million 'hits' on the Internet, emphasising the growing international interest in its symbolism.

8. *The Sculptured Rocks*

In this design you petrified the language of your soul-
Your own symbolic logic;
Linked a little world with universe,
Arrested time with space.
You saw the cycle of your birth and death with clarity
As sun and moon spun round,
As buds burst into leaves and fell upon the nourished ground.
A rhythmic pulse beat out like water flow,
Rippled from your centre to the stars.
The living rocks bear traces of belief,
Knowing all you used to know.
The curlew cry spills out
A plaintive, bubbling message to the moors
Above the desecrated graves and broken stones
As it has always done.
Its curved beak swings down from the sun
To execute parabolas in heather-scented air,
Or sink in silence to an unresponsive earth.

Prehistoric rock art at Old Bewick, over 4000 years old. (Birtley Aris)

The ruins of Blawearie House are prominent in a moorland landscape, providing with its trees and former gardens an oasis of tranquility and interest. It provokes powerful feelings, often influenced by the seasons.

9. Blawearie House

Blawearie like its name is tired of life.
A ruined farmhouse stands among
A broken patch of green.
Nearby are sunken trackways sunk in mist.
Among the giant rocks
Are little bits built into walls
To pen the sheep,
Where, once, the shock of death came strong:
A sheep, fleece rustled by an angry wind,
Neck trapped in fallen branch,
Stared sightlessly from empty skull.

On hills and slopes around
Dull cenotaphs of far more distant death
Upheave dark crusted molehills from the earth
Or mouth their rings of teeth
In silence at the passing clouds.
Where are you now, you makers of jet beads,
Of bronze, and arrowheads of flint?
A massive capstone covers up your head
As walled inside a cist you lie,
Knees underneath your chin.
Back to the womb, your mother called to you by name;

The posture of your birth and death the same.
I cannot shake the sadness from this moor
Where I have watched the rainbows
Leap across a blackened sky –
A covenant between the light and dark.
More than the hand of man has swept away
The fragrance that belongs to life.

Before a scarp drops sharply to the west
A table for the universe is set
Where sunset pours its colours into circles
Spinning round the centres of their lives,
Or empties silently the radiating ducts.

Pause for a while upon the ramparts
Of an Iron Age fort;
Follow the sunsink down across river's red
To towering Cheviots ahead, now crowned with mist.
Do not look back.
Blawearie turns your heart into a tooth of stone.
Alone. Eternally alone.

Blawearie House before its final collapse (Birtley Aris)

10. Blawearie House

In 730 Holy Island was insula Lindisfarnensis, and Lindisfarenaea in 890. It could mean 'the island of the people who travelled to and from Lindis', the name for north Lincolnshire.

11. Lindisfarne

I have been lifted far above the clouds of morning,
Slanted over landfall with shafts of evening light,
Breathed in salt-splashed air
That sparkles haloes to the shattered sun.
A gentle, flattened coastline spread below a wash of cloud,
Is broken by an island deep as it is tall.
There is a boat that hangs in space,
Masted with birch, with silken sails,
Drenched with a rainbow of hope.

Lindis is left far behind.
The call of a gull, wave-beat and lull,
Wreckage of lives resisting the pull
Of the sea from the shore are no more.

This silent water hides the thrust and pulse
Of purple jellyfish around a broken base
Of basalt columns growing in the sea.
A Viking's bloody axe pursues
The eager eyes of missionary priests.
A sacred script with inlaid gold
Moves among drowned hands of weed.

Above the moonrise and the leap of stars,
The kestrel's stillness, curving curlew's flight,
A crucifix of cormorant drying out its wings,
Lies the lost heart of Lindisfarne.
The land of Lindis lies somewhere
Beyond the prow that now I point
Away from land, away from all security
Of places with a name.
The same now
As it was when travellers came
To name the Isle of Lindisfarrne

Lindisfarne to the mainland

The Lindisfarne Gospels are one of the most respected and beautiful works of art in the world,, and were made by one man on the island of Lindisfarne, later to be called Holy Island.

12. *Gospels*

The ultimate devotion, conviction,
Absorption in the wonder of creation,
An urgency of conveying messages of hope
Of resurrection of the dead and spirit:
The Gospels proclaim bright light
To banish superstition, save us from the depths
Where Grendel waited to emerge
To tear us limb from limb
In hatred, from the protozoic slime
Rising from no-hope, ignorance, bestiality.

Jarrow and Lindisfarne were giants of a new-born age
To keep alive the flame, scatter fell darkness,
Some through words and some through art.
People were offered beauty, hope,
If not in our world but in that to come.
Images lived on;
Keys and frets, trumpets and spirals
Borrowed from another world
Threaded the beauty of the Word made Flesh,
A background and an integrated flow
Through pictures of Apostles and their signs:
Matthew, imago hominis, man with wings,
Imago leonis, the lion Mark,
Winged calf, imago vitili, Luke.

Imago aequilae, John the eagle
Put all the emphasis on a human face -
The only way the Gospel could be taught.
Cross-carpet pages shocked the eyes with
Art beyond our comprehension, wrought by monks
In stone-built cells.
Only the best was good enough for God,
So gold leaf had to be acquired,
The finest colours, jewels and richest skins.
Eadfrith, superhuman, crafted all himself
On Lindisfarne, the wonder of the Christian world.
That island was to fall to Vikings' bloody rage
And yet its art and message still endure,
The flame burns on,
Miracle of preservation.
We keep a special admiration for initials
Crafted to perfection:
The interlace, energy perfect in control.
Mathematics of sublimity,
Epitome of human patience
Harnessing the dance to crafted certainty

A replica copy of a page of the Lindisfarne Gospels in Hexham Abbey

St. Mark (Lion Symbol)

One characteristic of Celtic art is a pattern of interlace.

It survives particularly well in stone, such as crosses, and is famous in such manuscripts as the Lindisfarne Gospels. Its effect is lively, like a well-choreographed dance.

13. Celtic Dance

Bold interlace, extended sinuosity,
Grows out of stone, of wood, of paint, of vellum,
Living out its life in memory
Of wooden ships that breast pulsating waters of the northern seas
Drawing up from many fathoms of the deep
Those monstrous beings born of men's imaginings,
Trailing fronds of seaweed from their fins,
Their jaws, their scales that glitter far below the reach of sun.
The curved whale's back, a dragon's spiralled breath,
The slip and glitter of swift fish are buried deep,
Waiting to reach the surface of men's minds.

From water now to air, to clouds
That dance to wind-song as the sun
Slots beams amid the swirl and chase of this high restlessness.
Light breeze fills sails above the dragon prows
Plays with the rigging slack and tight,
Pushing ahead, becalming all at will.
A wooden keel grates on the pebbled beach
Where foam fills gaps in writhing back and forth,
Its sea snakes hissing, seeking out new land.
Waves follow, rolling crests down to the shore

By power unleashed, tugged by pale moon's gravity.
On shore, trees tangle branches high above invaders' heads
Filled with the possibility of serpents lurking for the kill,
Their tails curled round thin stems
Or holding other creatures for support.

This is the stuff of interlace, of restlessness
Tamed to some extent by men, a metaphor
For inspiration, understanding, knowledge of a past so deep
That all must be imagined, dreamed.
Pagan the symbols, Christianised by guile, for continuity,
Weaving tendrils, leaves, grapes, snakes
In patterns where God is the vine, his people are the branches;
Source of red wine to drink in memory of death,
Made stronger by the blood of Crucifixion:
This is my body, this my blood.
Remember me.

The wayside crosses carved from wood or stone
Stand as reminders of this sacrifice and praise.
Stone can be cold, unmoving, yet the images
Have life of their own, a work of centuries.
Crafted to perfection:
The interlace, energy perfect in control,
Mathematics of sublimity,
Epitome of human patience
Harnessing the dance to crafted certainty.

The small Duddo stone circle is a survivor of a circle erected at least 4,000 years ago. This poem was spoken as part of an ITV visit there and broadcast on site.

14. Solstice: Duddo stone circle

On such a night the hills dissolved
And re-assembled in a shifting mist,
Numb with moonlight's touch.
We learnt that silence was not hostile,
Took upon ourselves its deepest strength
Waiting for dawn's layered sun.
A moon that paced
As crow's shout cracked the sky
Fled from the triggered bird-song
Hesitant, then loud.
Before our eyes, a second birth,
A new-created universe,
Green and blue and gold.
Fluted stones whose shapes had shifted
With emitted heat
From bearded barley heads,
Buried to the hips,
Reclaimed their circle and identity,
Introspective, Janus-headed,
Guarding and inviting
As the sun's diurnal course
Played a slow game
With shadow shapes
Time and time and time again.

An important part of prehistoric landscape and life was the erection of circles of standing stones, varying considerably in size. Northumberland has only a few.

This poem sees them in general.

15. Standing Stones

Rooted teeth, the hunter's hold on flesh
That once roamed free
Pursued by points of flint
Broken from the ground and shaped.

We need to rearrange the universe
To suit ourselves;
To drag stones, sometimes shape them,
Plant them in the earth
In rows, in circles, single sentinels
Enfolding, leading, isolated,
Each according to our need.
The circle pulls the sun and moon
Down from the rhythmic flow of sky,
Ensuring that their magic works for us.

Stone rows lead the rising and the setting of the sun,
An avenue of our own creation,
And when crops fail, beasts sicken,
Fever strikes and children die,
Our faith is vested in recycled rock
Born of the earth but pointing to the sky,

Invested with acknowledgement
That without god's assistance
We are but specks of dust, and powerless
Within the vastness of a universe.
Stones, planted properly will help our crops to grow.
Stones guarantee the flow
Within bow's reach or slingshot's range
Of beasts that clothe and nourish us.
When nature fails us,
Bringing death, disease, the breaking up of tribes.
We do not blame the stones,
But offer them new bribes.

Standing Stones (Gordon Highmoor)

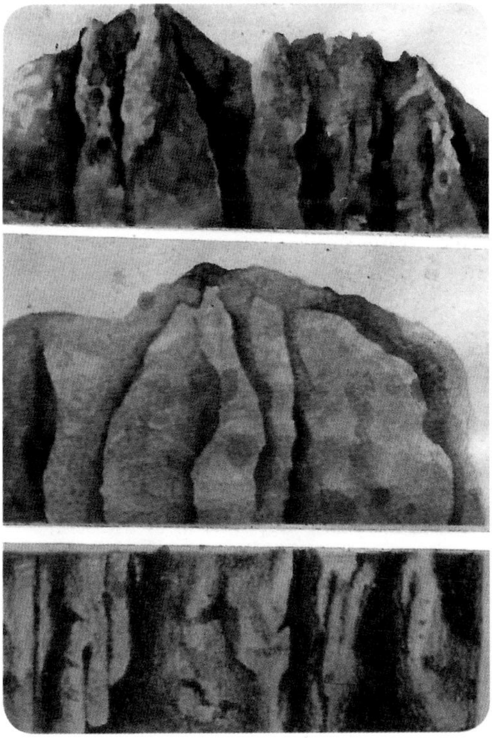

Low Cleugh bastle

This is one of many small fortified buildings that provided borders with some protection against raids, but not against armies.

Northumberland was Border country, its northern limit the River Tweed.

Safety for the Borderers lay not in governments, but in the clan system, where loyalty to a 'surname' ensured some protection along with obligation.

16. Reivers

Names like Armstrong, Charlton, Crozier and Hall
Were Border families arranged in clans
According to their names.
A law unto themselves beyond the Wardens
Who would curse and hang them for their crimes
Or find it in their interests to encourage them,
They formed the Mafia of the North.
They burned and stole at every chance
And no one's farm was safe.
Sometimes it was the policy of those who governed
To encourage anarchy and strife;
Real law was thrashed out among thieves.
Yet people loved, were not perpetually at strife,
And when the time was right
And kingdoms were united with one Crown
A peace began to grow.
So, as we walk the Cheviots and Simonside,
Or climb up Warden Hill, visit Fallowfield
In peace and quietness,
Sometimes a jet will scream above our heads
Reminding us of turmoil in a not-too distant age.

The site of the battle of Flodden, apart from a cross on Piper's Hill, does not stand out as the last big battle site of war between England and Scotland. The fields grow cereals in abundance and the area is generally calm. I would often take courses from Ford Castle, (where James 1V of Scotland spent his last night before he was slaughtered with many of his nobility on Piper's Hill the next day) to the battle site. On this occasion it was the anniversary of September 9th 1513.

17. Flodden Field

A lonely piper played a lament
Over the field of Flodden
When rain eased for a while,
Leaving wet hawthorn berries
To cry rich drops of blood from crowns of thorns
Over the unreturning men-at-arms.
This boiling battle, hand-to -hand
Ordered once by kings, with lairds and lords,
To feed ambition, lust for loot,
Adventure far from home
Ended in one vast burial,
Blending bone and sinew with the earth
Which held their bodies for a while
Until they were stripped of everything:
The spoils of war.

That piped lament beneath a granite cross
Erected to the brave without a label of nationhood
Contrasted with the crazy dash of modern horses up the hill

To celebrate catastrophe, all shapes and sizes
Both of horses and of humans on the run
To reach parked cars and cans of beer.
Dignity, not celebration should have marked that fatal day.

Piper's Hill from Branxton churchyard

From Humbleton Hill to Monday Cleugh and Yeavering Bell

The Cushion Dance often came at the conclusion of Kirns, or harvest, dances. It goes back to Elizabethan times, and was still performed in Northumberland early in the 20th century. Part of this poem includes the verbal ritual, word for word. One example of this custom comes from Great Ryle, now a very small settlement.

19. The Cushion dance: Great Ryle

When the candles in the old barn
Had nearly burnt away,
We rested weary backs against sweet-scented bales of hay.
'The Cushion Dance, The Cushion Dance,
Before the break of day'
Was what we asked the fiddler,
And he began to play.

They placed a cushion in my arms,
My blood was laced with fire;
The barn swung round above my head,
I stumbled with desire,
And laid the cushion at your feet.
Deep silence filled the byre.

'This dance it will no further go'.
'I pray you, good sir, why say you so?'
'Because Joan Sanderson will not come to.'
'She must come, whether she will or no.'
A silence fell as she knelt at my feet.

Around us the ritual chants were complete:
'The best bed, the feather bed, the best bed of a';
The best bed i' wor hoose is clean pea straw.'

The candles in the old barn had nearly burnt away.
'Welcome to you, Joan Sanderson'
Was all that I could say as I raised you from the cushion
At the dawning of the day.

Hadrian's Wall from Housesteads to Cawfields

The Roman frontier, east to west from sea to sea, means many things to many people. Some see it as a triumph for the Roman army and others as an acknowledgement of defeat. It became a convenient quarry for building stone. It now attracts thousands of visitors, as it is not merely a wall with fortifications, but a structure that takes advantage of varied and exciting scenery. What the soldiers thought of it is another matter, and we shall not know.

20. Hadrian's Wall: Housesteads

A place where empire halts.
Mist-haunted desolation holds in check
The will to move ahead.
And soldiers' eyes uneasily survey
Vast northern wastes;
An end to conquest, like a fire
That fades; but embers glow
And can be fanned into a flame.

A regiment of stone.
A geometric pattern coaxed from rock and soil,
Or forced persistently with toil.
Something to wonder at, admire;
Triumph of discipline
Ordering a landscape to obey.

Shut out the cold,
Stoke up the hypocaust,
Bring in our standards and our gods.

Each turret, fort and castle on the Wall
Becomes a reassurance of a different world.
The sound of marching, whiplash of command,
The clash of interlocking shields on alien soil;
Reaffirmation of the glory that is Rome.

Our hands rough--cut with mortar and sharp stone,
Legs stiff with pushing loaded carts through mud,
A finger broken on high scaffolding,
Thumb crushed by mauls in rock--cut ditch-
These were the lowest prices that we paid.
We joined the Legions, and we fought,
Became the masters of the north,
And our reward, as we are dwarfed,
Crushed in the shelter of our wall,
Housed in our barrack--blocks, patrolling roads,
Or dicing all our pay away
Is to be part of ranks on ranks of stone,
Cut to order, bound, by harsh winds flayed.

When I am dead
No one can really take my place.
This Wall will crumble, have to be rebuilt,
Fall down again, be quarried for its stone.
Yet I am part of it.
I lie in the foundations of a road,
Or feel the warm breath of calf in byre
Or watch a visitor admire the remnants of my work.

Northumberland was one of the earliest centres of Christianity in Anglo-Saxon times, known universally for its scholarship, evangelism, and works of art. One such early centre was at Hexham, and this poem imagines what it was like for local people to be faced with great changes as the surveyors moved in to plan what became known as the finest church north of the Alps.

21. Hexham: The Forerunners

Out of the river mist we saw our landing site,
As wild geese broke the silence with their hurried flight.
A curling thread of woodsmoke shimmered from a dark, coned roof,
Carrying a scent of fragrant cooking drifting towards fields
Won from woodland clearings and from burnt-out scrub.

We hauled our raft ashore and toiled along the track
That led from riverbank to settlement.
Rough farmers stumbled down the slope to meet with us,
Fingering their spades and hoes in challenge to our right.

'We speak for Etheldreda, Queen, and for your new lord Wilfrid.'

Such words had their effect, there was no one to dare
The voicing of a disagreement with the power of Church and State.
They knew the limitations of their role in life.
Theirs to plough, to till, to sow, to reap the harvest of their toil;
Theirs to secure the boundaries of fields,
To keep their beasts from harm in pastures close to home;
Theirs to protect their wives and bairns;
Theirs to obey, or break out in a rage

When what they built up, what they loved
Was doomed or under threat.

'We come in peace. We bring good news.'

Could any news from that far land of Church and State be good?

'You have a chance to walk with God, to build His temple in this place.'

We had already made a choice of land to build our church:
There on the hill, flanked by the streams that fed the Tyne.

'Hagustaldesham, now famous in the eyes of men
Is where you share the glory and the power.'

That's what we told them, yet we knew
What all the coming changes meant to them:
A higher price for food, a ready market close at hand,
Work in the quarries, work to fashion stone,
Work with timber, jobs for all at home.

They wanted to know more; we squatted in their dismal huts,
Stared at by finger-sucking bairns
And drank the proffered, bitter brew.
We told them of the plans, the wondrous transformation of their land,
Of Wilfrid's vision of the rising church
To meet God in the clouds of Hexham's skies.
We offered gifts, for we had come prepared
And knew before we left that soon from miles around
The hunters and the herdsmen, farmers, those with skill
Would make their way from hills and woods and fields
To do God's work, and benefit themselves

Hexham Abbey crypt

The Hexham 'cathedra' is a stone seat made when the priory was built in Anglian times. It was a bishop's throne, and became a place of sanctuary for those who were fleeing from the law.

22. Frith Stool

The Frith Stool in the Abbey bears a little of this interlace,
Formalised into a trinity of dependent curves.
The solid block of stone, a bishop's throne, sags to seat
Part of a body-shape, polished with use,
Now almost split in two, filled with a hoary serpent in the crack
When renovation, changes to a plan, forced it to be moved,
Making it vulnerable.
And yet the seat is fitted for the hips
Pressing with a curve the solid stone,
Forcing the occupant to sit with unsupported back,
Arms spread, flat palms that force a dignity of judgment and control,
Part of essential, demonstrable power.
This is an invitation not only to respect solidity,
To accept the power of hierarchy,
But to dance a little with restraint, for edged images have that life.

The monastery of Hexham was built, and was splendid for its time. It was to become a centre both of control and evangelism It also shared tumult, destruction and rebuilding with many other Christian centres.

23. Anglian Hexham

Before the burning of the Priory nave
Result of savage war between the English and the Scots,
A replay of the sacking by the Viking hordes,
There were some periods of peace;
The land around was farmed,
The Market Place was where the people came to trade.
People were drawn together by a common bond,
Living upon each other's labour to survive.
Most are the nameless ones
Whose lives are not recorded in our books.

Upon a platform high above the Tyne
The Augustinian Priory rose
With blossoming of arches springing from
Their fluted pillars like a song of praise.

The Canons went about their work
Of serving God,
Were buried in the graveyard when they died.

And deeper back in time
The church that Wilfrid built from Roman stone
Plundered from abandoned forts along the Wall,

Was such a lovely and a wondrous thing
That it was called the finest building
North of Europe's Alps.

The power of minds, the influence and wealth
Made this a place to wonder at.

But in this town
We look at a kaleidoscope of change;
Each part can tell a story,
Throw an image on a screen,
When past and present
Hold the future in their hands.

Destroyed by Viking raids, Hexham suffered with other places the horror of attack. The Norman Conquest brought Anglo-Saxons into subjection, but after short periods of peace, the Border between England and Scotland was seldom at rest as it seemed to suit England and Scotland that way. The Borderers suffered from attacks by both sides. This poem takes the Scottish raid on Hexham Priory as its theme.

21. The Scots: Border Raids

They poured along the valleys from the north
Like molten pitch, burning, destroying all before their way.
The Scots rampaged; a bloodlust veiled their eyes,
And they forgot the child they murdered could have been their own.
And they forgot despair of crops destroyed,
Of butchered kyle and slaughtered sheep,
For what they did was in a different world.
Damnation for their deeds returned in sleep.
For they would see the Priory burn,
The desecration of the cherished bones,
The beauty of creation broken down,
Destruction of the house of God,
Destruction of the people's town.

At their retreat they left a broken dream
And real lives lost to butchery and greed
A smoking heap of ruins laced with human bones.
Blood will have blood;
The English were to do the same
And back and forward armies marched

As people on the Borders caught the blast
Of hatred and of politics gone mad.

The nave became a graveyard for the town,
Bones piled on bones, covering Saint Wilfrid's crypt.
It waited centuries, for a more enlightened, peaceful age
To clear away the horror and renew the nave.
We are but dust, and must to dust return,
But we are the fire of inspiration that will burn
To recreate the town of Hexham and House of God.

Hexham Abbey during a candlelight concert

The following poem was recorded for Margaret Howard's Classic FM radio programme about the annual Abbey Festival, which uses candles throughout and ends with a Candlelight Concert of great beauty.

25. Hexham Abbey: Candlelight

Enter. You meet prayer-soaked stone
Invested with soft light, broken by stained glass.
You meet wood, warmed with time,
Darkened by caring, polished by use.
You meet images in paint:
Hollow-eyed Death, presiding over
The dance of the feckless and unsuspecting.
Here are lines of bishops and saints
Stretching in strips, with snatches of story.

Time spins and spirals all in one blend.
Brittle fragments of the Empire that was Rome,
Bundled Gothic pillars, black-edged in strong sunshine shafts,
An order of mind transformed to order by hands
That wield chisel and mallet.
Arches glimpsed through arches,
Soaring out of sight, upwards,
Light lingering on light.
Shadows shifting, corners hiding.

Listen now.
Bass from deep-throated organ pipes
Rends the foundations on which arches lie.

Light notes float among the curves
And thread among patterned stones.
Add candlelight: the melting shapes
Make tableaux of their own,
White stalactites, winged angels,
Birth and crucifixion all in one.
The soft, light touch of candle flame
Strokes the arch's throat, bends pillars inward.
Golden clerestory holds its shadows on a gentler rein,
And human faces are transformed
By wonder and an inner light.
All things conspire to lift the soul above the earth
From which this Abbey grows.
The tiny parts fail by themselves to move;
The way they blend
Disturbs us to the roots.

Sunlight in the Abbey, before the sculptures were re-located

26. Sunlight in the Abbey

Sun spilt upon the golden harvest of her hair
Against dark vaulted wood
That led from nave to chancel.
Here was the crossways,
Where feet echoed on stone slabs
Above the deep-dug crypt.
She was alive and filled
Stone and wood with
The colour of her movement.
She stood awhile
Where God's insistent light
Linked her to heaven.

Flat on a flagstone floor
A lady and her knight in stone stared heavenward.
As if in answer to their pleas
God's sunlight shattered through
To stipple stained glass life on still limbs.

God's sunlight did not burn.
A cross glowed gold, flanked by flowers.
Saxon interlaced and interlocked
Its complicated shadow shape.
Fluted pillars fountained arches
To a peak, pointing to a world
Beyond this stone, beyond all art.

Below, encompassed by this shell of stone,
Pale faces caught the passing light
And shared the mysteries of those now dead.

27. Pilgrimage End

A pilgrimage ends, in a way, at the place where we began.
Yet we are not the same when undertaking it.
We have been filled with visions of a past
That is no airbrushed picture,
But an encounter with reality.
It challenges all that we mean by Art,
All that we think we stand for,
Linking us in a great chain of being
From origins to achievements.
So much of our Northumberland is spared
The worst that time can ravage, though not untouched.
We spin in a timeless vortex,
Sucked through visions of what has gone before,
Our feelings heightened, senses honed
To see beauty and meaning as we grow
To love, to feel, to see, to touch,
To be a part of that great timelessness
Into which our parents gave us birth,
As they were born of parents long before.
We learn the merits and the vices of humanity.
We carry in our hearts so many images.
For me, a Northumberland Evening which carries on the Pilgrimage:
After thin rain, warmth of evening sun.
Prismatic brilliance
Of every drop that hung upon
Each softened curve of leaves' lips down.
A slanting searchlight
Startled every intersecting branch,
Tipped and topped the trees
And skeins of wild geese threaded endlessly

Across the darkened sky.
May we love our landscapes, protect them from exploiters
And leave our children and their children with a marvellous legacy.

Ending of the journey

Thanks

To my editor, Kim Cowie, for her sympathetic and skilled handling of the text and illustrations.

To Helen Clark, my granddaughter, for her artwork, and to my friends Birtley Aris and Gordon Highmoor for theirs.

To Joe Cowie for his photo of the Angel, and to Newcastle University for the Middleton air photograph.

To my son, Julian for helping me with the computing.

To all those who have read and commented on the poems so helpfully, including David Bell, Vera Mutimer and Sonja Bailes.

To Christopher Mayer and Christine Blance for their recording of my reading, that helped me so much to assess the music of the poetry.

The cover was designed and produced by Helen Clark, who also designed the mural at Alnwick bus station of the Alnwick Castle Garden treehouse.

My thanks to Northumberland National Park and to Stewart Bonney of 'The Northumbrian' for their support.

Thanks to Anna Jackson, Wilf Stone andTom Macmillan for the music at the first public performance of these poems, and to Toni Bush, Owen McArdle and Roger Highnam for their readings.